It Was Fever That Made The World

PHOENIX POETS
A Series Edited by Robert von Hallberg

It Was Fever That Made The World

Jim Powell

The University of Chicago Press | Chicago and London

THE UNIVERSITY OF CHICAGO PRESS, CHICAGO 60637
THE UNIVERSITY OF CHICAGO PRESS, LTD., LONDON
© 1989 by The University of Chicago
All rights reserved. Published 1989
Printed in the United States of America
98 97 96 95 94 93 92 91 90 89   54321

Library of Congress Cataloging-in-Publication Data

Powell, Jim
  It was fever that made the world.

√ (Phoenix poets ~~series~~)
  I. Title. II. Series.
PS3566.08323I8   1989   811'.54   88–20720
ISBN 0-226-67706-0
ISBN 0-226-67707-9 (pbk.)

Contents

The Crooked House

It Was Fever That Made The World

It was fever that made the world
burn last summer, that afternoon
when I lay watching the sun pour
its incurable folly slantwise
into a plum tree's crest,

infusing it till the whole crown glowed
red as infected blood translucent
in a syringe. Sunlight was
the carnal fuel leaves burned for life—
obedient to hunger,

they turned their faces toward it
with such greed, in their recklessness
I could see fall's wreckage breeding:
motionless, each leaf swarmed
with an earthly fire

commanding as the power I felt
churning inside me last night
listening to a guitar rant
dirty blues till the crowd eddied
open as everyone

started dancing: past will
or withstanding, in the hot dark
song after song grew stronger, thriving
like summer in our shaken limbs.
Outside, between sets,

after midnight in the sidewalk
company of strangers, all
the flushed faces reminded me:
sweat was a fever sign last June—now,
my drenched shirt cooling

felt like health, like strength, urgent as the sight
of taillights queuing at the tollbooths
Friday night, then streaming up the bridge
till all five lanes of their sharp reds merge
toward the city's bright towers.

Home Free

In the documentary one scientist
tells how, with the same skill
that let him help to make that light,
he used the angle of blind-slats
whose shadows had been burned
into a schoolroom wall
to calculate the altitude
of detonation and confirm
that the device had functioned as
it should above Hiroshima.

The low October overcast that leaned
above the blacktop and torn
grass of our playground a generation
later seemed to conceal a weight
that would soon fall on us.
In ordered drill we entered
the huddled smell of sneakers and
eraser dust till the All Clear,
crouched in our shadows where
the desks were bolted to the floor,

and late that hot fall afternoon daydreamed
over arithmetic
we would survive into an aftermath
of freedom, the bomb inaugurate
a frontier of long orchards
and no parents calling:
there, we could be wild Indians
prowling behind the vanished fences
of a new suburban wilderness
we'd riot in all night long.

But in the chronic sky of real dreams
big as a Thanksgiving Day
Macy's parade balloon, Khrushchev
straddled a bomb-shaped zeppelin bareback.
Its prop drone cut across
the sleep I ran from, wrestling
to escape. No longer himself,
he came to manifest a figure
fixed in heaven before he came
to wave his sickle down at us—

like Kronos, who ate his newborn children till
Rhea fed him a stone
instead of Zeus, father of light
and degeneration. Zeus handled him
as he had Ouranos:
shearing his genitals
with a flint sickle, he flung them out
over the sea and took the gods' throne
(but from the waves he'd broadcast with
red seed, some say, Aphrodite was born).

It was easy, later, to think it made us different:
we could call ourselves
the first to ripen toward the light
of a general annihilation
we could believe we shared
and wore like a mayday crown
of paste and paper roses: if we imagined
its bright burst always above our heads
we'd cast no shadows, like the children
absent from that schoolroom wall

becoming exemplary—like Khrushchev
dismembered in our nightmare.
Making a shelter in that difference
we came to terms that set us free
not to remember where
we stand, which rescued us
from every denouement until
those terms became our story: Trust
nothing, we said, to the next day.
It might not come. We dwelt on that.

Revisiting The Haight

That year, sea-fog in tufted hanks
spun through the eucalyptus tops
below our attic flat,
thick coiling strands that looked as if
they passed right through the limbs—intact—
torn along the Panhandle toward the Bay
in the wet salt wind as though

mist and branches inhabited
worlds separate as that warm room was
from the winter weeks outside:
only damp darkening the leaves
at first, to show the two had touched,
and then the fogbank lowered, settling over
their slippery, peeling trunks.

Parchment scraps of their bark littered
the summer grass this afternoon
where I walked, looking up
five stories through those windows, trying
again to bring nearer to mind
two friends I lived with there twelve years ago,
and caught a glimpse, instead,

of a self I'd barely recognized
in our company of dwindled figures
rushing out of sight
as I saw that in twelve more years
torn along in the same wind
with every solid thing today housing my life,
this insight, too,

will shrink and darken to another
almost unrecognizable story.
The shock was like the moment
when last month's earthquake had kept up
long enough to let me watch
the walls and wonder if they'd crack, break open,
fall—then longer, enough

to know myself helpless, freed
from fearing a titanic power
so far beyond my stature
it was without design. I think
that's what I wanted, last night
in your arms—to be caught up beyond design
and sheltered in that wind:

hidden, escaping, safely and well
lost to all but our limbs and glances
tangling till near dawn
—and instead, slowly discovering,
inside the moments our attentive
pleasures open into immensity,
my small self meeting yours.

A Letter

Dear Lowell,
        Berkeley had its first fall rain
this afternoon: droplets still shine along
the plum tree's wrinkled twigs outside my window,
at rest in their forks or clinging to the curled
edges of leaves dark as the cabernet
pressed, casked, aged and poured from grape clusters
harvesting now seventy miles north of here.
Five months ago those branches shook thick plum
shadows against the pane, swayed with the shouts
of children out of school who dropped their bikes
below the limbs they straddled to take all
the fruit unripe.
        I put on "Nessun dorma"
to remind me: while Puccini's last
tenor aria overwhelms the soundtrack
of Jack Hazan's film, the artist runs a long
stainless steel kitchen knife into his painting
—atonal soprano rasps from its parting weave
score the crescendo as his shaking white
knuckles lock on the canvas to tear through
the figure of his lover's painted face
because it wasn't true.
        Later, he'll start
over, darker hills from the south of France
for his background, and leave a space pure white,
its clear-cut vacancy outlined for the loved
image to occupy when he's composed it
from thirty snapshots taken one afternoon
in Kensington Gardens: each locks the boy
in the same awkward pose, as if the lens
looked and looked at its model, trying to find
and fix the one he looks for when he turns
so stiffly inward.

Watching the painter's hands,
I thought how one I meant to love would not
stand still inside the likeness I had made
but broke out of that settled clearing to
become another person and swept through
everything I felt true like a dull scythe
over and over
                    till the simple world
of darkened windows, quiet streets and sidewalks
quailed in the clear double ranks of slowly
counted lampposts, as if in their sharp line
nothing could hold its ground but took cover,
and what I walked in were the travesties
I kept in mind to people cryptic regions
only desire inhabited. Every named
and graceful thing they stood in place of fell
silent.
            One night, coming home late, I thought I found
a present in the mail. Then I knew what it was,
and forced a laugh at the gross craft staining
immaculate cardboard with just my address
and, in large electric-blue block letters,
"FREE GIFT"—watched myself watch its missing name
provoke stumbling fingers to tear it open
and find out at once what I knew already.

But it wasn't soap I smashed against the wall
in sudden, silly, furious tears because
it was only a bar of sample soap.
'It was only a pictured face,' I wanted
to rant back at the artist in the movie,
'not the gift you looked for'—and with that want
from memory I filled the shape left white
and waiting on his canvas, on the screen.
But when we watched it together, it seemed another
entrance—unprojected, gratuitous—
opened between us there,

                         both taken in
to an aria in a language we can't speak
and almost understand, always just out
of reach and moving toward us—like the song
inside Tom Constanten's "Dejavalse."
I think it was almost this time of year
I first heard that ragtime American
slow country piano waltz, its tune so strong
the words to marry it seem just ready
to rise half-heard inside each passing note.
I've tried to catch them half-a-dozen times
but I can't quite get them right.
                         They'd say that
close friends around a table, good dope,
talk shared till dawn in a kitchen over wine
after the party's left, can last awhile
making a place to rest beside the stove
that outburns every dark and cold, outlasts
all of the busyness that breaks and breaks
our circles. The words call me there and know
the promises they give aren't kept and say so
in the tune's lilt and braggart sweetness, its
forgiving mockery.
                         Now the friends
I think of to recall that scene have scattered:
one's gone to Italy, another's here
but distant, I've quarreled with a third, and the house
and stove were sold. In German, one of them told me,
'gift' means 'poison'—that must be why we call
them 'free,' to think that what we take does not
constrain allegiance. A free gift was what
I wanted, given like the sun that sinks
unseen above the slow plain mass of clouds
hunching from sea to foothills:
                         through a strip
cleared in the west it strikes full on the Bay,
hammers that choppy steel to one wide sheet

of blinding light where Alcatraz lies anchored,
a black cut-out battleship, guns trained
on the Marin headlands. If you were there
tonight you'd hear foghorns whose calls describe
the distances where real ships move and pass
under the bridge they can't see from the water
yet know is there: a phosphorescent ghost
swept by the steady, circling scan, its shadow
fills their dark screens.

Thinking of you in Paris,
I imagine a trail of down and pale skin running
clear from your throat to the blondish tuft below,
a sign our bodies share as if to keep
the memory of their first cell's division
that constitutes us separate and whole
and leaves this mark no other scar effaces,
this condition of our custom with the earth
where our uncertain calls and answers start.

Heat

Everyone else slept and we
were skinny-dipping in my mother's pool
when the moon rose and birds

sang for high summer in a valley oak
whose seedling I mowed carefully around
twenty years ago.

Back in Berkeley the next day
light from the water where we troubled it
still glanced back from the leaves, a look

of recognition on each changing face,
and the tart fume of just-cut grass that lifted
from the park recalled

that morning's cool persuasions,
dew clinging in the brazen glare of noon.
It was as if that shore

where all forgotten things will find their lasting
home was never lost or touched by need
but day by day was spared

for our return—as though, downtown
where a half block of stores burned to the ground
last month, the damp of ashes still

inhabiting the air (full, rough
feathered at the back of my tongue) coaxed
a thirst for nothing else,

just the thin creek barely
moving in the shadows under a bridge,
to shelter there and watch

sunlight slice down between the planks and rule
sharp lines across the stream, marking its passage,
and to forget the time.

A Drink Of Water

I was edging along a deer trail
past halfway into a thicket so dense
the tarweed stains never washed out
of my jeans, but I almost turned
and backed out when I smelt it

thickening through the head-high bristle
of sage, buckthorn and manzanita,
smothering their alert tangs.
I must have been fourteen, and I'd never
known that reek, but my body

knew it and answered—nausea
was a kind of foreknowledge.
Sick sweet, and worse on the other side,
inescapable as the heat: there,
near the shade at the withered

edge of the clearing I'd broken into
a dead calf slumped into the soil.
It had nothing to do with me:
back in the brush, I'd fallen behind
the hunt so I had to hurry

down canyon again—step quietly
through brittle grass and keep watch
for bucks asleep under tanoak, black
oak, live oak. But it was so hot
long before the arroyo

bottomed out I'd forgotten the hunt,
forgotten the ragged hide
—even the flies had left it—sagging
to show its emptied bones, and the brown
grass blackening with decay.

The jeep met us in creekside shade
near the mouth of the gorge, an ice
chest in the back. But soft drinks
weren't what I wanted, or even
to sneak a beer with my cousin:

that August the creek still ran
wrist-deep, cold over slate-blue stones,
slow enough for the sky and branches
to stain it, flecks of dark amber oak leaves
rusting unstirred on the bottom.

One night lying in bed years later
when you were five thousand miles away
I swear I saw your two eyes large
and wet in the light above me—so present
there that everything else

vanished as I was taken wholly
into blue-green flecked with amber
that was also a stream and shade
and my thirst slaked. For a long time now
I've wondered if that was the night

you tried three times to hang yourself—
furious at failing, at the cheap
French cotton cord that broke and broke.
But not till tonight did I recognize
the stream I thought I saw

in your hallucinated eyes,
or remember the hunt it ended,
or the dead calf. It's been six months
since we broke up. Memory,
recognition quench nothing.

Inscriptions

a Letter, for my sister, Kath

You won't see them when you're there this summer—
preservation's winter work—but the artisans
I watched restoring all those Paris churches
last December, up on their tarp-draped
scaffolds moving quietly under the opened
span of a dome, reminded me of you
and how you're learning to restore the body.
And though perhaps I only had in mind
a phrase that calls our flesh the soul's temple,
I kept remembering how one night you told me
that once you'd gotten over the sickening
estranged familiar feel of cold thick flesh
folding back from a scalpel, what you found
most amazing in Anatomy Lab
wasn't the way white sinews bunch and gather
clean-flayed muscles in translucent sheets
and lace them to the bone, or that the heart
for all its careful chambers and passages
proves simple: even more than matching slides
of others' blood cells against your own to see
a difference you can describe (though why
yours vary none of your doctors understand),
what most drew your attention was how the coils
and crevices disclosed after you'd sawn
open a skull slowly bewildered you—
that this grey paste your scrubbed and gloved hand weighed
so easily could be where everything
we call ourselves takes place. But the charts
you study map so small a part of that
sparking synaptic maze that our conversation
went threading that night toward the unsurveyed

reaches where neurophysiology
can't answer for a soul: it's hard to think
that memory, reflection, imagination,
passion, all the stories we tell ourselves
as if we chose to take them for our own
might be just patterns written in a fire
so quick some buildings and most trees outlast us.

In Paris, where the arches draw perspective
from repetition down the aisle, then pivot
around the choir, in dusty chapel bays
lit by the wavering long flames of votive candles
you'll sometimes find inscriptions cut in bronze
or marble tablets—cracked and patched ex-votos
that testify to a child cured, a husband
brought back to faith, (one purchased by a student
who'd passed his *examen*), but most remembering
the powerful or learned dead. Summed up
in Renaissance Latin elegiac couplets
or revolutionary French, their lives
are worn exemplary phrases, pious lies
that tell the truths of what their authors wanted
others to think—yet pathetically in earnest
now, slowly spelled out in the poor winter light
centuries later, as though the lasting stonework
whose shelter they took settled to add its weight
to their witness of the mason's trust
that everything once lost is simply lost
and so, while it can, must be recalled in stone,
that crumbles slowest.
                            A friend of mine just left
for the Sierras on a dig; last time
her group unearthed a miner's tongueless boot,
two dented lanterns that still keep a whiff
of kerosene, and several red iron spikes—
things harder to read than funerary inscriptions.
But the same narcissism calls her back, I think,

as kept me reading them—or keeps you,
after your lab is over, imagining
the convoluted flesh inside a skull,
hoping to uncover some cursive imprint
down a digressive path worked through grey matter
to conduct you past the dissolution
of its lethal earth. That's why my friend's
eyes and curious touch are so drawn to
those railroad spikes: though they bear the signs
of their long burial through the heavy years
since a blacksmith tonged one from the forge,
clamped it down on the anvil and raised his hammer—
half-gnawn by the wet earth, each flanged head shows
the careful print of his sledge blow still, and something
of contact with his fabricating hands:
a rusting incarnation of his will
lodged in the soil like a splinter in the palm
and dug out as a token for the time
that others of our kind have left, lost or planted here.

Gnostic philosophers thought Christ Crucified
the image of such an incarnation—man's spirit
hung on the body's cross, about to be set free—
and read, inscribed on all things, the signs
of an informing will that made the world
make sense as it gathered toward its final sentence.
But the polychromed torment carved in wood
and nailed up in Paris churches always holds
the same pose: belly knotted in
above torn and knotted rags, chest
sagging, head tipped back to almost touch
the shoulder, he looks up to heaven just
the same as you look up at him constantly
suffering the pathos of his inadequacy
to lead your gaze into the empty air
below the vault. Its arches, like his arms,
insist we know the weight they've lifted from us

is more than we can bear, as if to say
that you and I have trespassed into flesh
and need a warrant for transgressing here
—as if we could escape its earthly margins
free as a pigeon's shadow across stained glass,
and still survive to contemplate some image
of that freedom.
                          When I was three or four
our grandmother (the one whose name you bear)
left me waiting beside a stuccoed pond
in the half mission style, half moorish entry court
of a store in San Jose while she went in
to buy a lamp. Under the heavy sun-glare
there were goldfish: pale-gilled sluggish things
in butter clouds of light, that wouldn't move
unless I tossed a rock into the pool.
She asked me afterwards, had I been throwing
stones at the man's fish. It's the first lie
I can remember telling, and somewhere while
I sat, smaller in the backseat riding home,
an old man in a beard opened his heavy
book to a page where he first slowly inscribed
my name into the blank sheet, then X'ed
my fabrication there—writing things down
to make them happen once, until we are
wholly engraved . . . and another grandmother
hurrying six inches at a time
across the apse, shifting a carton full
of groceries for *M. le Curé*
from arm to arm, bends her intent grey bun
over the votive candles. With the same quick
turn of her wrist as when she's pulling weeds,
she wrenches those burned down to thumb-length stubs
deftly from their sockets and blows them out:
it's time to leave.
Distracted, businesslike in a much-washed
housedress strewn with geometric sprays

of small blue faded flowers, to me she seemed
like death, that blows out all the candles it makes
us burn, half hoping we'll discover something
other than darkness thrust back in their glow,
half longing to escape that light, in which
we stand defined.
               Still, I can't close this letter,
I suppose, without an image of the soul.
Others at other times, I know, would pick
differently, but because you'll soon
be going there yourself, today I'll choose
a statue called *The Venus of Arles*—just
as she stands, twenty feet from one high wall
in the enormous public space of the Salle
des Cariatides at the Louvre, gazing
reflectively down at a marble mirror
broken away a thousand years ago,
only its handle left now in her grip.

Lighting The Furnace

Each evening now the ash blue flame
swept from my fingertips
climbing its gas ladder up the flue
burns more the color of that single earring,
one of the pair your father

left you, lost in a crack now
somewhere under my bed
lodged out of reach—its jade bead
the size of a bird's eye among the splintered
rubble of wrenched beams

and plaster when this house is finally
pulled down: small hope of shining
then, warm on a flushed cheek—no matter
if its story sticks, garbled in old men's
gravel throats, the rumor

of a love long since interred,
or if its gold pin pricks
some gardener setting irises, thick hands
too numbed in the cold soil to feel his bead
of blood lost there: blue flowers

will greet him from his yard that spring.
This winter, nights will be colder
with you gone. Each evening now these jets in flame
climb reaching from my fingers to be consumed
and vanish with the day.

Sappho: To Aphrodite

Artfully adorned Aphrodite, deathless
child of Zeus and weaver of wiles I beg you
please don't hurt me, don't overcome my spirit,
        goddess, with longing,

but come here, if ever at other moments
hearing these my words from afar you listened
and responded: leaving your father's house, all
        golden, you came then,

hitching up your chariot: lovely sparrows
drew you quickly over the dark earth, whirling
on fine beating wings from the heights of heaven
        down through the sky and

instantly arrived—and then O my blessed
goddess with a smile on your deathless face you
asked me what the matter was *this* time, what I
        called you for this time,

what I now most wanted to happen in my
raving heart: "Whom *this* time should I persuade to
lead you back again to her love? Who *now*, oh
        Sappho, who wrongs you?

If she flees you now, she will soon pursue you;
if she won't accept what you give, she'll give it;
if she doesn't love you, she'll love you soon now,
        even unwilling."

Come to me again, and release me from this
want past bearing. All that my heart desires to
happen—make it happen. And stand beside me,
        goddess, my ally.

Song

Dear eyes, slut eyes
my angel for tonight
suddenly your glance
above a hand cupped full of matchlight
across the roaring room

and now this compact
of our locked gazes—promises,
frank craving:
once, I saw this same lust at first sight
in the blank marble stare

of a Roman statuette,
the god Pan sodomizing
a billy goat:
a fixed, feral leer so naked
it looks innocent—Pan's thighs

intent; the kid's beard
pinched in the god's right hand
and his head tilted
back to return that gaze, a mixed
look on the goat's wise face

of quizzical
detachment, and some
curiosity
to contemplate these ephemeral
ecstasies in the god's eyes.

Baudelaire On Love

I believe I have already remarked in these notes love's close resemblance to torture, or to a surgical operation. But this idea could be developed in the bitterest style. No matter how much two lovers are taken with each other, abounding in mutual passion, one of the two will always be calmer, less entranced than the other. He, or she, is the surgeon, the torturer—the other, the patient, the victim. Can't you *hear* those sighs, the prelude to a tragedy of dishonor—those groans; those cries; those gasps? Who hasn't uttered them; who hasn't—irresistibly—extracted them? What worse could you find in the torments applied by the most meticulous torturer? That spellbound, gone look in the eyes, and limbs whose muscles spring out and stiffen as though under the impact of a bolt of electricity: drunkenness, delirium, opium, among their most frenzied effects offer nothing so fearful—nowhere such strange cases. And the human face, that Ovid thought fashioned to reflect the stars, now able to convey nothing more expressive than this look of insane bestiality—or slackened, relaxed in a kind of death. For surely I would commit sacrilege in applying the term 'ecstasy' to this species of disintegration.

—Terrifying game, in which one of the players must lose all self-control.

Once, I heard the question discussed: in what does love's greatest pleasure consist? Someone, naturally, said "in receiving"—and another, "in giving oneself." "Ah, gratified pride!" was the latter's retort—and the first: "lewd humility!" All these 'sensualists,' these talkers, sounding like the *Imitation of Christ!* Finally, there was found one rash utopian who argued that love's greatest pleasure resides in creating a new generation of citizens.

Me, I say: the unique, love's supreme passionate gratification lies in the certitude of inflicting *pain*. Both man and woman know, from birth, that in *evil* is found all pleasure.

Napoleon Reviendra

some ironist has scrawled
across a Metro wall in cherry lipstick—
one more savior set to rise again

returning north from exile
like the sun toward spring—and on the train
from Fontainebleau to Paris, in the sallow

January rainlight
the hedges veering off through stubble fields,
their leafless brambles drained to a shade of cinders,

looked spent past any chance
of rising to another year's exactions:
exhausted at the prospect of insurgent season

beyond season always ending
here—cowering insensate, cold in the failing light,
bogged down in the mud and snow on the road back

from Moscow. But nature's sex wars
spare *them* foresight: overcome
by the simple compulsion of the sun

they bud again and flower,
sap-swollen tendrils leafing to embrace
the same infatuate exuberance

this year as last—incapable
of sickening at the spectacle of their own
repeated willful yielding to blind need.

The Crooked House

This is a lacquer tea tray
my father brought from China.
Home sick in bed from school I'd eat lunch off it,
in convalescent daydreams uncovering
an inland sea with islands

ideogram junks sail home
across its wine dark calm
enamel surface—each character a cage
of golden brush strokes, skeleton hull
and bamboo battened canvas,

each splay of shining bristles
capturing one touch,
one gesture of a hand no more than bones now.
And there's a rickety pagoda teetering
from the tufted headland

where one craft returns
bringing gifts to close
the gape of absence and perpetuate its scar
—a ramshackle rustic temple, though a boy
lives there: he goes fishing

from the skiff, dangling his line
inside the curling, beveled
edges, and overlooks the floating wreckage
of estrangement and the scene that takes place here
I can't remember—but why,

over and over, peering
from the threshold of this room
I've backed into, why must I construe
this single sentence? Must I settle down for keeps
inside this crooked house?

Fire Signs

The Weaver

Inside the four-square heavy oak-beamed frame
that supports his loom
in one corner of a cold grey-plastered room
the weaver sits alone.

He smokes a pipe, and does not see the hand
his gaze rests on, left motionless
on the shuttle, or the cloth emerging from it
like a broad scarlet tongue.

He wants to feel content, but each knot
is a broken thread bound
into the fine, smooth web. His life outside
this room is snarled and ragged.

If he could only sit inside his loom
as his brother does, at peace,
intently dreaming what will have been his time
into the careful fabric,

he would not notice how these walls remind him
of the blackening snow
shoved to the cobbled gutters he'll walk along
toward home this evening, and stop

and light his pipe again and watch the smoke
curl from the glowing bowl
and then resume his work, sitting alone
in the open cage of his loom.

after Van Gogh

A Glass Blower

A Woman Watering

She leans away from the soft spray
fanning off her thumb,
the green hose snaking out behind her,
wanting to hold in mind
only the pole bean's waxy creepers

threading upward among their tripod's
weathered redwood-stake legs,
and where the sun already reaches
into her garden, leaving
clean shadows on the clean soil

she's worried into gentleness,
the way its light aligns
this cool morning's clarity,
its *charity:* bright water
catches on the air and mists,

drifting from her hands through leaves
outspread to receive the day—
slow small gestures uninflected
by their own enormous
fragility: easefully indifferent

to her nurture. Cooking breakfast,
she'd watched the fine white sand
in spirals draining through the hourglass
pinch of an egg timer
mother left her, its model watchtower

squinting at her from the stove:
promise transfixed in memory
as the grains eddied into the narrow—
she could almost hear it hissing
that the world's garden absorbed her soul

only in its own vanishing.
But *this* garden, these plants
were their own lives growing: not hers,
not made to consummate or mask
her wants—and this was water, not sand.

*

Mare's-Tails

From the sinkhole bottom the sky
was a perfect hard circle of turquoise
too bright too far above her turning there,
tricked back slipping down
its mudslick throat, into the sopping pit

again with her long blonde hair spread
streaming on the water, warm currents
coiling it brushing against her arms, her throat,
the green pool gushing
at her lips, and in her eyes prolific summer

weeds up its steep banks in clumps
uprooted where she tore them, climbing
out before. But the long grass was too slippery
now, and thigh deep
underwater thick downy silt kept clinging,

sliming her bare legs to the crotch,
the mare's-tails blazing overhead,
wild strands combed out to icy points in flight
across its narrow turquoise
mouth stopped cold: an invulnerable virgin calm

sharp as though scratched on hissing glass,
impassive above her thrashing there
exhausted, caught in quicksand, gasping water,
letting herself go—
the easeful fluent ooze sucking her down

and under. A bird in the house
slapping against the pane
above her pillow woke her: the squeak
pressed from its muffled breast
rebounding from the glass, its frightened wings—

she threw the window wide open
but it flew out another way
and dozing off she puzzled at her dream:
was she the grass and the sinkhole
and her own life turning, there in the pit, to sand?

*

Broken Bottles

The blowpipe's iron shaft
was warming in her grip
as she dipped it to the crucible again,
stirring its flanged lip
in the slow pool to take up another

gather of glass and blow out
a pear shaped bulb, waving
the rod's tip lightly to lengthen it a little,
this wobbling balloon
of incandescence thicker than raw honey:

elemental orange,
swarming, ripe with heat.
For this vase she wanted something sidelong,
the turn of its milky turquoise
neck diverging toward the lip aslant

like the crooked limestone nose
of that paterfamilias, that Roman
citizen she remembered sitting in a doorway
at the Louvre: that wry skew
between those eyes steady with contemplation

and the set of his mouth
not stoic, just done grieving
for the knowledge that what made him who he was
were his scars. Glass vases
were calm silent things, and she knew her bent

for reticence was something
she learned at home, averting
submergence in her mother's furies, in the icy
undertow of coerced
reconciliations: this aloof,

impassive mask now stuck
so tight it made her ache
and her idols—measure, formal necessity,
poise, grace—all fabricated
before she knew what fabrication was

to make herself invulnerable,
calm enough to face
her mother stirring at the stove, beef stew
steaming in the ladle,
and not betray she saw her nourishment

doled out in measured doses,
each one exacting
commensurate recompense of gratitude
in obligatory poses—
and all struck in her mother's image:

all poise, all promise, too
brittle underneath.
But she would break herself of that and find
the peculiar skew she wanted,
or let the vase's throat find its own bent

in the annealing, absorbing,
healing trance of work:
while the glass was molten, shining on the pipe,
it had almost the freedom
and luxuriance, the shapelessness and profusion

of water: working it was slipping
into the green sleeping river,
it was Coltrane blowing soprano sax, molten
improvisations pouring
from the bell and fusing in the crucible

it was ripe Nile mud's original
black solar alchemy,
metamorphic confusion among the slimed roots
of reeds and sand—and glass
was made from ash and sand and broken bottles.

Captives

*By this you may understand, my dear Johannus, that a Roman
gentleman a few days ago in one of his vineyards in Rome at the
place called le Capoce near the Church of St. Peter in Bonds, not
far from the Amphitheater, discovered three figures in Parian stone
in a subterranean chamber of the greatest antiquity, splendidly
paved and inlaid miraculously, a chamber that had been walled up
by the passage of time.*

Letter, third week of January, 1506, author unknown

A vintage of stone in the vineyard that day,
up from the chambered ruin locked in the earth
    beyond reach of plow-blades
so many years;
         And Michelangelo
    is said to have come within hours
picking his way through the drift of clods thrown
back from the pit, the pale flesh of vine roots
    torn in a frenzy of excavation,
        turned to the winter sun—

After so long a time (dust sifting through cracks,
slow loam gathered on ruin, forgotten)
      you must dig deep, past
where grape roots have probed, generations,
to reach these roofs, pry up the still-level stone,
    open this gate in the earth
and descend to a pavement whose tiles
—where the sun penetrates—glint up
      a mosaic through rubble:

    In the pool's smooth mirror
        gathering poppies
           to set in her mane

Demeter's priestess Nikippe
        paces beneath green boughs
Where the sun eddies silver
        against poplar leaves
                and the depth sips light like amber:

"Keep your blades from the cool grove
        Our Lady of Sheaves endows with fair breezes.
Send home this drove of slaves:
                they may not tear branch and quick root
To feed stoves, fence cattle,
        stave your halls against heaven.
On other trees she allows
                you to glut your cruel axes.
These woods, Erysichthon,
        are the share of the Goddess."

Later, he squats in the margin,
        the king's son, Erysichthon,
                who felled trees once
In that forest, now begging
        for crusts at the crossroads
Where hunger has dogged him,
        wasting, a wax doll
                in the sun

—mosaic stone, smooth and flashing through wreckage,
still largely buried as Michelangelo
        steps through the debris
to walk in a palace sunken for centuries,
enter a room whelmed in the field's dark,
and run his hand over those anguished stone limbs.
        Pliny was wrong, he said:
not from one block of Pentelic rock
        they cut the *Laocoön*, but five—

the eye of the master
              knowing its seams:
not ignoring the cry
                    throttled in stone
nor the boy's thigh, relaxed,
          smooth with dying,
but seeking beyond them

      a jointure of cry and craft
where the old story unfurls from cold marble
freed again in the light pouring over the threshold
      torn in the hillside.
                        While green shoots rise
from each stump the prince left and the stained pools clear,
dissolution had raked the shapes Michelangelo studied,
      coiled them, pastured, and passed on:

          father and younger son,
                  missing right arms;
          the elder,
                      wrist and right hand.

      In the vault where the afternoon
half reaches, thrusting thin shoots of sunlight
through shade, his fingers slip over the stone,
          trace out the gnarls time scrives in those faces.

Their memory will dog him through his long death watch:
Wrestled from torn rock almost thirty years later,
      his *Captives* fail to break out of the blocks
where his chisel frees them, harvesting stone
          whose flesh will not melt.

                    for Florence

Time And Light

for Mark Goodman (1951–1980)

I

Leaving our cars to stand
beside your grave, we enter a place
where sunlight englobes us, pulsing
as if drawn toward shape on a potter's wheel
and that shape destruction,
an unmoved whirlwind where traffic
beats against the Rabbi's last words.

An astroturf dropcloth
laid on the mound to keep
from our eyes the mass of black earth
that will bury you folds back;
shovels enter to take
their part: locked in the space
ritual clears, we are making an end here,

standing around a hole,
and cannot leave while the form lasts,
and cannot leave. Gathered about
an emptiness like a vessel where time
has stopped, the rite
carries us who are here
becalmed and swallows you in its shapelessness.

*   *   *

Some life not part of yours
hungry to make

more of its own wrong kind
eats at yours from inside till

crowded back into
a small dark

you cry out for your mother
to warm it—

a cry you would have
forbidden yourself

in life.

"Photography is time
and light:" you said, "that's all

I need."

*   *   *

Calling to say you were dead
Lucie told me this morning
you came back at the end
out of confusion to speak

of flying into the green
wind outside a Matisse
window where your gaze would dwell,
the print you taped to the hospital wall

taken down now, and us left
still saying "Mark," still
calling a name that you don't
answer, now sounding its silence.

*   *   *

Spring earth scattered on oak planks
and the peacocks whose generations still
stray through these well-kept outcast grounds—
your eye caressed what it saw, drawing it out
into the light, and the camera remembered:

slowly circling an unfilled grave,
the precious borrowed Bolex at your eye,
you danced so the opened earth would reel
and shudder, gaping out of a nightmare screen
while Puck's damn'd sprites troop home to churchyards all:

peacocks and an open grave wound in a maze
of passion sweet blind children dream—
Bottom the Minotaur of Love,
such brightness in that transfiguration,
"I am amaz'd, and know not what to say"

standing again among these tombstones
after eleven years, come this time
to see you buried in the earth
you filmed, and hear again the shrieking
peacocks harrowing the summer haze.

II. *Graveyards, Monuments, Underworlds*

Founding their great stone cities, our ancestors
plowed a line in the dust where walls would rise
and at each future gate to knot these borders
    with ceremony and due rite
    made human sacrifice; and Joseph
the Arimathean set bounds to another field,
buying the plot where they laid him down,
the cave hewn out of rock and the great stone,
    and opened a gate in the hillside.

    But what place can you find in this tale,
or any we might make? That city of god
grounds on refusal and founders. Turning to think
of death, I turn to the world and lose you.
    The gate cut in the hill's flank
    opened on loss and stands, still
empty, a boundless field where nothing roots.

Yet if I could imagine you've joined that light
I saw once (even that seeing learned, I think,
    from your vision), an act of attention
    sustaining like sunlight that slants
keen on the river woven by evening winds
    and hones the edges of wavelets, bright bounds
        moving in order,
    inks black their troughs
        in flowing inverse
of motionless, deft recurrence . . .

On swamp land in the trough between three hills
the separate hearths that gathered on those heights
    settled their common dead, and when
    priests came to plow round the limits
and bind three tribes to found one city
they made that graveyard its center—a space cleared
and still held by their unacknowledged dead
    where the city's speech would rise,
    its trade thrive, Rome's first forum.

*   *   *

All the stories of that dark,
a space set apart that is no place,
are told not in the crypt but here
where we bury at high noon—
making a rite for the day light,
a hole for you in imagination
that has no site in worlds we share
and leaves all underworlds one ground
where you are lost
                         and we remain
as if death solicited a script
to name the faces we adopt,
our wardrobe of poses struck
over your grave.
                         What's told is lost
to language; not told, lost to itself.
We fall between. Into this hole,
this rounded *not* that's never filled,
our words drop—dust, now, of a field
we set aside for death and keep
for our avoidance. Each of us
consumed in our own ends, we find
no common ground to mark your loss.

*   *   *

Now in the tight trench you go
down beyond shadow at noonday, footsteps
            lost where the long slope
quickens you downward, shouldered on
through the swarming dank and mute trampling
            down where the bloodless press close,
bone white dice in the massive cold and formal hysteria
where forgetfulness rules the Death Lord's gaze,
his sunken island and iron horns,
            his eyeless bride,
you go down
to be lost in a waste of burning cities,
            Dresden, Gomorrah, Dis:
there, haze gnaws at the rust air and communion ends—
there, still pools cast no light back to be lost.

III

From your movie projector the white sheaf
would open its cone into the darkness,
petals of color
falling to meet the screen.
Light changed to shadow and flowed there,
in a fullness, under our gaze, as the flowers,
peacocks and an open grave
now transmuted had moved once under yours

in this heavy world our fitful imaginations
feed on, play over in blue flame:
the alien light
where we dwell most, always
about to overflow and find
rest in a place answering our desires
—a bright pool that reflects
lips always about to meet their thirst.

That's how it must have been when you finally knew
you were dying, knew you would dwell
in that light's
expansion no longer. The grace
of speech that holds us withdrawn,
falling back into this world to stay, did you reach
desire's unchanging end—stuck,
meeting yourself at last while the light burns through?

In The Desert

Once in the night
we were falling

with the whole earth
heavy beneath us

away from the stars
that fell toward us

at the same speed
into a loneliness

our singularity
birth gate to grave

and that ungentle
darkness opening

gathered our falling
like cupped hands.

Circe

All the new young men
have come to crowd around her knees again
and lean toward her lips,
sitting bewitched at these feet their grandfathers
once nuzzled with drugged snouts.

She is old now, and beyond them,
but her face still feels their eyes, her transparent hand
remembers girlhood
and flirts the white frail wisps back from her cheek
as she resumes her stories

of Odysseus: how he tamed her, left her,
then returned—his voyages, his works, their last
long few years together.
No need of philters to transform them now,
no need to subdue them,

these young men with their bright eyes
craving entrancement: her own eyes are brighter, welling
quiet hilarity
from springs replenished where her body's age
can't reach. Fragile,

not weak: his praise her strength, his jewel
of glory in the Muse's crown her laughter
delighting to tell
how he subdued her—as if, remembering,
she possessed him still.

for Olga Rudge

Cleopatra

Let's order drinks; let's
    dance for our liberty,
our land, our lives; let's
    celebrate glorious
long feasts at each god's
      image and
decorate all of their altars, Romans:

Before this day it
    would have been criminal
to bring up vintage
    wine from our fathers' cellars
while that queen plotted
    ruin for our
Capitol, mad to destroy its empire

in sick conspiracy
    with her corrupt, depraved
and castrate cabinet—
    wild enough to hope
for what she pleased and
    drunk with all sweet
fortune. But it diminished her frenzy

when scarcely one ship
    returned, saved from the flames,
and her thoughts, no longer
    crazed by Egyptian wine,
turned soberly to
    honest fears when
Caesar pursued her in flight from Italy

driving his oarsmen
        hard, like a hawk that falls
on gentle doves or
        a hunter after a hare
that flees through snowy
                meadows in
Arcadia—he, intending to put in shackles

that fatal monster—
        she, to die free, who felt
no womanish start of
        fear at a dagger blade
and though a fast ship
                waited, ready,
didn't retreat to some hidden country

but dared to look on
        her royal capital fallen
with clear, calm eyes and
        bravely take up the snakes
to tease their anger
                till they let her
flesh have a drink of their deep, black venom:

emboldened once she
        had decided on death,
she scorned the ship Rome
        sent to carry her back,
a queen no longer,
                to be led in
glorious triumph, a woman, still unhumbled.

Horace

Heights

a Letter, for Paul Lake

There's a hawk in the distance of the postcard
you sent me of the Ozarks, towering
against a gap between two thunderheads,
so far away I think whoever took
the picture didn't notice—busy capturing
those clouds blown eastward full of sun, their shadows
small and sharp on the bright grass of clearings
deep in the forests that spill down to flank
the valley as it winds legendarily
into the haze. But these muted hills don't fit
your menacing description: the camera makes
their invitation simple. Still, behind
one saddleback I think I can imagine
the kind of devious gravel road you write
of driving, mapless, running out of gas . . .
an unmatched pair of ruts first cut by wagons
following the canyon's pliant lead
from halfway up its slope, around each shoulder
easing into another shaded draw   ˙
then out past broken fences and flat across
some brush-rank field toward one more string of switchbacks.
Its course accommodates the shifting ground,
compliant to the contours that it scars
and lends what definition ironshod wheels
could leave behind
     together with new names
that came to stay more slowly, and still inhabit
down weathered local roads—where you look out
the lie of the country that you've come to live in,
listening for its stories. But if they tell
of outlaws, poachers, fugitives who wait

just off the road in constant ambush, night-hunters
with rank bait and flashlights to draw the game
almost to their muzzles, wild mountain men
dynamiting the creeks to bring fish bobbing
stunned to the clearing surface and scoop them up
by the gunny-sackful, perhaps that's not
to show themselves unneighborly, still less
to shed a violent glamour on their forebears'
unbuckskinned shoulders—but to suggest (these
outlandish figures raping Persephone,
their exaggerations in our place)
how tenuous the order that whole families
over generations have imposed
upon those hills still seems: and, by comparison
with that exemplary mayhem, to excuse
the slower, more purposeful, and deeper scars
they know getting a living from the earth
leaves daily.

        Here, November's thinning out
the leaves, and soon the city lights will hang
again among my neighbor's walnut branches
—now, its prolific summer crown, though falling,
still obscures them, as if to show that leaves,
though yellowing more rapidly than paper,
take natural precedence and will survive
to supervene and darken those bright hills.

One clear night last summer I could see
three celebrating cities launch skyrockets
over the Bay. San Francisco fired
so many, out past the Alcatraz light,
I kept mistaking its five-second sweep
for the glare of another lift off. More burst
above a plane of lights between two trees
that's somewhere in Marin. And much nearer,

as if higher, the rockets spouted brightest
from the Berkeley Marina, rose into flame
and settled toward the water, out of sight.

I knew those fireworks meant to commemorate
a time when the roads cut westward first diverged
into a wilderness now truly virgin
because no longer claimed for anyone
before he took it for himself, cleared it,
and held on, till there was little left to take.
Like other holidays, that one declared
that when the earth in its measured revolution
around the sun returns to the same place
and all the stars converge to make the same
map of the constellations as presided
over that first day, ceremony can
suspend the season with its mortal leaves
and as if no further passage intervened
revive the original story and the time.
But to me the rockets seemed to celebrate
a revolutionary origin
less than they marked an anniversary,
a benchmark for endurance showing how
old that story has grown, and by what force.

Still, as I watched the rockets rise and burst
and tried to guess which city fired each shot
I was surprised, overhearing myself recall
the names I could, how each name drew me outward
thinking over a route to take me there
across the landscape that they spread between them
as they settled into their seasoned places
on the periphery of their future legend's
limited terrain. Together, they made a country
(inhabited, familiar, much smaller than
the continental power they meant to honor)
where I could move freely among known things,

and at the same time, described its boundaries
and closed it: and that sign of limitation
seemed, oddly, part of the liberty disclosed,
almost the way sometimes from a summit
the horizon will look higher than you are,
as though you'd hiked an hour along a ridge
to come through to the top and look out from
the highest point for miles, and found it at
the bottom of a clear blue bowl of wind,
sunlight and clouds whose rim the distance rounds.

But then, another evening, I went walking
in the hills above Berkeley with a friend
who talked about a six-month drunk in Saigon
in 1972. That year the war
was nearly thirty miles away. White Mice
on Hondas worked the streets by day, their justice
cheaper by the week; past midnight dog packs
—all ribs and teeth—gnawed at the tires of Jeeps.
There for cheap booze, cheap drugs, cheap women
and the spectacle of one more Armageddon
(he wasn't in the service), at night he'd stare down
into an alley from his flophouse roof
and watch grey rats swarm through what little garbage
other scavengers left, or look outward
toward the horizon. There, showering tracers, missile
trails, and the shell-bursts—first grown quickly huge,
swollen with clear white light, then more slowly
washed out into the dark again—created
beauties unmatched in his hallucinations.

That was ten years ago. It makes a good
story, now. But as we talked, the dark
spread slowly toward us: lights came on below

from house to house and, street by street for miles,
delimited a map we recognized
and followed till we lost it in the distance
and general glow rising from all the cities
that surround the Bay. A more spectacular
display than any fireworks, to him it seemed
finally just the intricate pyrotechnics
of almost divinely clever rats busily
usurping the perfect liberty of the night:
a restless conflagration fueled by lust,
folly, illusion, avarice, willful violence—
the lights around the Bay were scar around
an unclosed wound that only would be healed
if the cold black water at the center rose
and covered everything.
                          I could see
what he meant: from our outlaw height,
almost divine, the countless intersecting
threads of that brilliant network did look like
the windings of one penitential maze,
man-made, man-tormenting, that would close
around us as we walked downslope again.
And as we talked, I remembered reading
that eleven centuries ago long ships
rowed up the River Ouse: their oarsmen took
the town by storm and sacked it, then settled on
its ruins. Apportioning the ground, they built
new homes, bred swine, and laid out wattle fences . . .
for urban archeologists to find
ten yards below the pavements of the present
city of York—half-rotten Viking barriers
that modern property lines still follow exactly:
untransgressed, unbroken, inescapable.
And though they burned the Anglian town and raised
another new one on its leveled ashes,

Eborácum, the place's Roman name,
eroded to a single syllable
persists, still audible today in "York"—
as stubbornly surviving as those fences
or the legend of their builders' violence
or the Indian names taken by half the states.

Ten years ago, living in San Francisco,
on sunny weekends I'd take the bus, sometimes
with friends, sometimes alone, to Lincoln Park.
Behind the Legion of Honor at Land's End
I found a spot I wish I'd thought to show you
when you lived here, though perhaps you found it
for yourself: through hedges, past the signs
(a landslide zone; you're not supposed to be there:
each year a few go over and are lost)
—a hollow at the cliff's edge, sheltered from
the wind and cypress-shaded all day long.
Two miles outside the strait there, I could see
nothing but ocean. I could forget the city
behind me, and watch the surface of the sea
grow smooth and darken, out where the wind died;
listen to the waves thwarted against
the rocks fifty or sixty feet below;
count seals, their slick heads bobbing on
the swelling steel-green calm beyond the breakers.
I went looking for the spot last month
and couldn't find it—could hardly find a landmark
to place it by. The ground has shifted, or
fallen away. Everything is changed.
Not even a scar marks it: the cliff's lip
worn smooth again in the prevailing winds.

Snow Drifts

Look how the snow drifts
    flare on Soracte's slopes
—there, straining branches
    barely sustain their white
load. Locked in ice, streams
        buckle, send cracks
stuttering over the winter's stillness.

Unclasp this cold, stir
    flame in the embers, pile
the hearth with fat logs.
    Bring out a bottle warm
with a summer four years
        gone, wine that grapes
drew from the sunlight on Sabine hillsides.

Leave the rest to the gods:
    once they have overcome
storm winds and strewn dead
    calm on the restless sea,
black cypress, old ash
        never stir, rest
still as the shade in Persephone's groves.

Today, don't ask
    what tomorrow may be:
whatever time chance
    gives you, put down for profit;
and don't reject love
        now you're young, don't
break from the ring where you dance with linked hands

while grumbling old age
keeps its snow from your hair.
Now while you still can,
in the cafes, through parks
and plazas hunt out
gentle whispers
under the cover of evening's short hours

and welcome laughter
from intimate corners,
the girls who hide there
giving themselves away,
and rings or bracelets,
charms snatched for love
tokens from fingers that hardly resist.

Horace

A Ghost

Ghosts do exist; death does not finish everything:
    some shadow lasts beyond the fallen pyre.
I thought I saw Cynthia lean above my pillow
    though she lies buried now beside the road,
while through my bed's cold kingdom sleep followed in
    love's funeral, and hung back, and complained.
She had the same hair as when they carried her away,
    the same eyes. Her dress was singed into her side,
her beryl ring was soldered to her finger, and Lethe
    had just started to wear away her lips—
but her breath against my cheek voiced a living soul
    as she clapped brittle hands and said:

"Faithless impotent lazy unspeakable coward,
    is sleep so strong it holds you even now?
Have the meetings in illicit streets we stole escaped you,
    my windowsill our nightly tricks wore down
where I shook out the knotted rope, swung over, hung,
    then came hand-over-hand toward your embrace?
Breast to breast at the crossroads—count the times we spread
    our cloaks and skirmished till the cobbles warmed—
all those whispered arrangements nothing but words
    the deaf North Wind tore to scraps and scattered.

But no one spoke my dying name. I might have held
    one more day captive if you had called me back.
What paid watch stood that night over my dead eyes?
    Your cut-rate coffin's pillow bruised my head.
Who saw you bend beside my grave, your black toga
    hot with tears? And if you couldn't bear

to go outdoors, you might have ordered my cortege
 to ease its breakneck gallop past your house.
You wouldn't pray the winds that took your promises
 to fan my pyre. No incense stained my smoke.
To scatter roadside hyacinths was too much trouble,
 to pour wine on my ashes and break the glass.

Crucify Lygdamus! Interrogate my maid!
 I saw her ambush in that darkened wine.
Let Nomas hide her poisons, burn their recipes—
 the white-hot iron will tell her hand she lies.
Once every public curb heard Chloris, your new love
 bargaining for her nights; now her gold hem
writes me letters in the dust, but if your maids
 speak of my beauty, she multiplies their chores.
Because Petale brought flowers to my grave she locked
 the pillory around her wrinkled neck;
she had Lalage beaten, hung by her twisting hair,
 for daring to ask a favor in my name;
she melted down my golden image while you stood by
 and drew her dowry from my flaming pyre.

But I don't mean to haunt you with your faults, Propertius,
 much as you've earned it; my reign in your books was long.
I swear by the Fates' song that no one can unravel
 —let Cerberus' three throats bark tamely at me—
I was faithful. And if I lie, may snakes couple
 upon my mound and sleep over my bones.

Twin habitations wait for us beyond Lethe;
 twin boats bear us where the stream divides
our mirrored passage—up one river Clytemnestra's
 adultery, Pasiphaë and her wooden cow—

but on the other, wreathed ships sail before the wind
    that bathes the roses of Elysium
where Cybele's bronze cymbals ring in the mitred chorus
    weaving faithful measures to plucked strings.
Andromeda and Hypermestra, faultless wives,
    narrate histories of the times that marked them:
Andromeda complains it was her mother's fault
    if cold stones and shackles bruised her arms,
and Hypermestra tells how her sisters cut their sleeping
    bridegrooms' throats—only she wasn't brave enough.
Thus we renew life's passions with the tears of death.
    (I suppress your many treacheries.)

If I have roused you now, if chance leave part of you
    still free of Chloris' potions, hear my commands:
Don't let my nurse Parthenië lack anything
    in her trembling years: she could have charged you more—
much more, Propertius; and Latris: don't let her hold
    a mirror up for any other mistress;
and those three books of verse you littered with my name,
    burn them: you've made enough of my praises;
and keep your lyric ivy off my grave—its tangled
    shoots grope down to twist around my bones.
But where Anio's apple branches lean to shade its stream
    and Hercules' spirit keeps ivory white
forever, carve these quick lines into my stone
    so hurried travelers from the city read:

HERE IN TIBURTINE EARTH LIES GOLDEN CYNTHIA
    AND LEAVES HER GLORY, ANIO, ON YOUR BANKS.

Don't scorn dreams come from the right gates: they stir
    over your sleep like shadow, but they have weight.

At night we wander: midnight frees imprisoned shades;
  even Cerberus throws back the bolt and prowls.
At dawn we must return: Charon rows us back
  across black water and counts each passenger.
Other women can have you now. Soon I alone will hold you.
  You'll be there with me. I'll wear down your bones."
When she'd prosecuted her elegy to this end
  the shadow slipped from my embrace and vanished.

Propertius

In Late March

Look how the sun's just
grazed the sea in the strait there,
centered beyond the bridge towers
like the bead in a rifle sight.

Last week that squat red
disk set over a palm's crest
lost to the south now: each day
leaves its blaze on a place removed

miles further, sets down
its full measure
opening toward July nights
where all the time in the world hangs

weightless, and takes one
more share of what's left till it turns
back from the north toward winter.
Still, tonight it's enough to watch

the moon rise, near full,
and pass over the sill, the eaves
—when it rains unmeasured light runs
down the branches' slow fuse.

Fire Signs

Our last ride that day
was a country doctor driving back from Denver
with a caduceus
home-painted on his station wagon door
and the backseat stacked with reading, Renaissance sculpture

and mystical philosophers
for the long southeastern Utah evenings,
who asked would we like to visit
the local artists' colony and dropped us out
down two miles of dirt road into the sage plain

under a dusty sandstone
scarp: stained on the hollowed rock face the shadows
of three torsos silhouetted
in blood rust ochre were slowly wearing off
the sorrel stone, the figure in the middle

broader shouldered, taller,
darker, the buffalo horns spread from his temples
sweeping their sickle arcs
above his escorts' bare heads. We made camp
against the cliff, gathered brush and railroad

scrap and piled a bonfire
huge in the clearing at their feet and watched
the third night crescent raised
like a scimitar against the cobalt evening
turn gold, then bronze as it sank into the haze

on the horizon. Night came
and then you danced in the late May desert air
naked under the naked
constellations, leaping between the shadows
twisting on the sand and the firelight leaping

bronze on your sweating arms
as you whirled three feet of burning 2X4
around you in each hand,
the lit ends spitting fir sap, flames torching out
on the wind you made, long sparks spilling off them

into the night. I still have
the photograph you took and printed in negative.
I can still make out
his horns, his fading temples, though you've been
seven years now among the sightless dead.

Between The Teeth

The black Labrador met us
again emerging midstream
as we were wading back that evening, his coat
soaked gleaming to his ribs
and his lips drawn wide in a dog grin

as he came trotting toward us
proudly across a tottered
granite outcrop, the same creek bed stone
the size of a drake teal
still balanced in his jaws, its mat black ovoid

cradled between the teeth:
behind us upstream
fir and pine branches were settling their chill
darkness across the pools
and spray and floating scraps of foam sent spinning

below the run of rapids
I swam toward that afternoon,
lurching buffeted through white water heaving
in its basin, then easing upward
slowly among snaggled glinting rocks, braced

against the veering weight
cascading into me—
and lay outstretched, wedged into the current,
sheathed full length in its lithe
pummeling: just my face on the churning surface,

almost all difference lost
between my muscles flexing
and the fall's supple lunges kneading them,
chanting to myself '*I*
am water I *am* water I am *water*'—

balanced between the rocks there,
lulled in that lisping tumult
I wanted to persuade you that what thwarts us
is recalcitrance to change,
not frailty, that we aren't so easily broken

risking falls as following
old courses wears us down
—and now here was this black dog again, the same stone
caught in his jaws like an answer,
its contours dark between his glinting teeth.

Housekeeping

After the old man fell
and broke his hip working in the garden
the shrubs next door grew free,
each year the pale new leaves
crowding denser shade against the walls

all summer, ivy over
spilling the eaves, the old couple both grown
too frail to trim it, and later
gone to a home and the house
left vacant, blinds drawn for nine months, then cleared out,

painted and sold. Today
when my new neighbors woke me, cutting back
the overgrowth, on the sill
beside my head dead bees
lay clustered—half a dozen, their dark wings

folded, their bronze fur
gold dusted in the sun on a white ledge
above the buzz and sudden
shriek of electric saw
teeth biting down on green wood, faltering

against a pyracantha
limb's sinewy resistance. At breakfast last fall
before they hung their shades
I used to see them through
those thorny branches setting up housekeeping,

arranging rooms, and once
that December when her mother came
to help them settle in
she sat at their back window
rocking her infant grandson in her lap

for hours—whispering over
his smooth head, or sometimes singing. I wonder
if his grandmother told him
as mine did me in her still
small voice that the law of this world is woundedness

and that all these shining
presences are put here for signs and keep
their secrets in the folds
of a fire enticing
as the wavering blue circles of gas flame

under the heater grate
down the hall, the ones lit there to blister
little fingers, ones
that grasp too greedily
and won't be taught to mind and not to touch

but look through semblances
to find the portents and commandments shadowed
there, veiled out of reach
of time. Virgil says
that in the underworld where each of us

suffers his own shade
our unborn souls are stung by such dire lust
to see the blinding daylight
that we swarm like bees
to drink the waters of oblivion,

furious to resume
the weight of incarnation and forget
past lives taking up
residence in new bodies,
helpless. Or cradling his oblivious bald head

in her arms did she gentle him,
nursing her promise with a song in her ragged
alto about the new shoots
that would be waving outside
in the breeze to welcome him this spring rolling

laughing on the grass
while in his father's hands beneath the eaves
the long bright blades
of the pruning shears are snicking
at the ivy, letting sunlight in at the windows.

The Piper

His lips' pursed embouchure
just perceptibly fluttering
and his eyes distant
above the seven reeds
of his Andean panpipes,

he lets his friends attend
to the business of Sunday strollers
passing, some stopping
to hear his purring low
notes' melody break free

and rise in fluent, calling
cries above their mandolin,
guitar, skin drums:
four young men traveling
to play Quechua folk tunes

in a windy civic plaza
far from home—no voices,
just instruments
spilling foreign echoes
off the neoclassic portico's

granite façade, and their
four faces silent in its shadow:
each the same
cheekbones, the same tilt
of jaw the precise angle

of Inca doorframes, stone jambs
tipped inward toward the lintels
of gates and windows—
alien, remote
in photographs of Machu Picchu,

trapezoid portals open
on emptiness in white granite
cyclopean
walls, their models still
visibly engendered

in these street musicians' skulls:
each of us the same, imposing
our own different
faces on the world
that shapes us our own skulls

and breaks or wears them down—
quickly or slowly, all
in the same wind
that carries off his pipe notes
rising in trilling runs

like water overleaping
stones and falling in bright
showers, a lavish
passing tune in praise
of what vanishes, not what stays.

Acknowledgments

In "A Letter" "Jack Hazan's film" is *A Bigger Splash* and "the artist" David Hockney; a performance of "Tom Constanten's 'Dejavalse'" can be heard on *The Waltz Project*, Nonesuch 79011. "Sappho: To Aphrodite" translates "Sappho 1" in the edition of Lobel and Page, with Lobel's emendation (*POxy.* 2288) in line 19. "Baudelaire On Love" translates "Fusées 3" in the edition of Le Dantec and Pichois. "Captives": On "Erysichthon" *cf.* Callimachus, "Hymn To Demeter." "In The Desert": *cf.* Rilke, "Herbst," *Das Buch Der Bilder.* "Cleopatra" translates Horace, *Odes* 1.37. "Heights": In GI vernacular "White Mice" were South Vietnamese military police (from their white helmets). "Snow Drifts" translates Horace, *Odes* 1.9. "A Ghost" translates Propertius 4.7.

Grateful acknowledgments to the editors of the magazines where versions of these poems first appeared:

Berkeley Poetry Review: The Piper, Sappho: To Aphrodite, Song, The Weaver.
Chicago Review: Captives, Cleopatra, Heights, Time And Light.
The New Republic: Sappho: To Aphrodite.
Occident: A Ghost.
Paris Review: Heat, A Letter, Snow Drifts (*Paris Review* 94); A Drink Of Water (as "Memory, Recognition"), It Was Fever That Made The World, Revisiting The Haight (97); Lighting The Furnace (as "The Beginning of Winter," 100); Housekeeping (106).
Poetry: The Crooked House, *Napoleon Reviendra*.
Scripsi: Heat, Home Free, In Late March, A Letter.
The Berkeley Graduate: Snow Drifts.
The San Francisco Sentinel: Song.
The Threepenny Review: Baudelaire On Love, Circe, *A Glass Blower:* A Woman Watering, Mare's-Tails, Broken Bottles, Home Free, Inscriptions.
Verse: Between The Teeth, Fire Signs, In The Desert.